CASUAL DAY HAS GONE TOO FAR

A DILBERT® BOOK BY SCOTT ADAMS

Andrews and McMeel
A Universal Press Syndicate Company
Kansas City

—— **ATTENTION: SCHOOLS AND BUSINESSES** ——

Andrews and McMeel books are available at quantity discounts with bulk purchase for educational, business, or sales promotional use. For information, write to: Special Sales Department, Andrews and McMeel, 4520 Main Street, Kansas City, Missouri 64111.

For

Pam "Why-Do-You-Sneeze-When-I-Talk?" Okasaki

Introduction

I was in the bookstore the other day, hiding in the back reading a new car buying guide, and suddenly I felt very ripped-off. I realized the book had no introduction!

This shortcoming was not mentioned anywhere on the cover of the book. In fact, I had almost finished getting all the information I needed before I even realized the introduction was missing. I felt violated. Used. Dirty.

I stomped over to the cash register, pausing only long enough to de-alphabetize some of the books in the kids section. (I do that because the children are our future, which can't possibly be a good thing, so I try to slow them down when I can.)

I waited patiently in line—to demonstrate that I am a reasonable man—then I demanded my money back. Predictably, the bookstore employee started spouting a bunch of "rules" they have about refunds. I discovered they are totally inflexible about the fact that the customer must buy the book before a refund can be issued. I argued that my ownership of the book was clearly established by all the yellow highlighting I had done. This logic fell on deaf ears.

I took a deep breath to gather my composure, muttered something unintelligible about "repeat business" and stormed over to the magazine section to catch up on my reading.

Frankly, I don't know how the bookstore stays in business with service like that.

But this ugly episode got me thinking about the value of book introductions. I realized that I have an obligation as an author to do more than just take your money. I also have an obligation to fill up a certain number of pages.

And speaking of obligations, there's still time to join Dogbert's New Ruling Class (DNRC) and get the free Dilbert newsletter too. As you've probably heard, when Dogbert conquers the world, the DNRC will form his elite inner circle. Everyone else, the so-called induhviduals, will be available as our domestic servants.

The Dilbert newsletter is free and it's published approximately "whenever I feel like it," which is about four times a year. There's an e-mail version and a snail mail version. The e-mail version is better.

E-mail subscription (preferred): write to scottadams@aol.com

Snail mail:

Dilbert Mailing List
c/o United Media
200 Madison Avenue
New York, NY 10016

S. Adams

http://www.unitedmedia.com/comics/dilbert

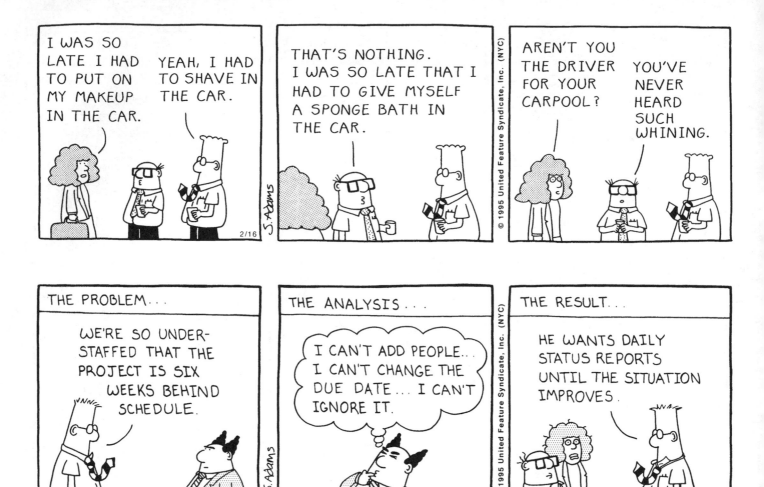

15

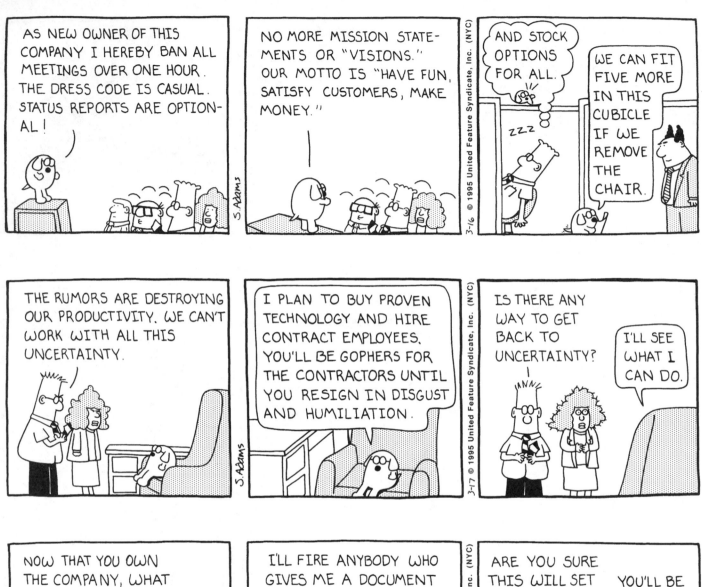

Panel 1: MY LAPTOP COMPUTER IS LOCKED UP. CAN YOU HELP?

Panel 2: REMEMBER YOU HAVE TO HOLD IT UPSIDE DOWN AND SHAKE IT TO REBOOT.
OH, THAT'S RIGHT.

Panel 3: I WONDER IF HE'LL EVER REALIZE WE GAVE HIM AN "ETCH-A-SKETCH."

Panel 4: DOGBERT THE CONSULTANT
YOUR BEST BET IS TO RELOCATE THE COMPANY TO RUSSIA.

Panel 5: YOU CAN HIRE ENGINEERS FOR TWO CENTS A YEAR!
IS IT DIFFICULT TO WEED OUT THE DUMB ONES?

Panel 6: NO. AND THAT LEADS ME INTO THE GOOD NEWS ABOUT THEIR OCCUPATIONAL SAFETY LAWS.
IT'S LIKE HEAVEN!

Panel 7: I WANT TO ASSURE YOU THAT ANY RUMORS YOU'VE HEARD ARE FALSE.

Panel 8: WE ARE NOT PLANNING TO RELOCATE THE COMPANY TO THE SOUTH POLE WHERE EASILY TRAINABLE NATIVE ESKIMOS WILL REPLACE YOU.

Panel 9: THAT'S GOOD BECAUSE THERE AREN'T ANY ESKIMOS AT THE SOUTH POLE.
EXCUSE ME, I HAVE TO MAKE A PHONE CALL.

S. Adams

© 1995 United Feature Syndicate, Inc. (NYC)

4-3

4-4

4-5

30

38

43

I JOKINGLY TOLD STAN IN MARKETING THAT I REPROGRAMMED HIS DNA. HE'S SO GULLIBLE THAT HE'S ACTUALLY CHANGING!

YOU MUST USE HIS GULLIBILITY TO REVERSE THE PROCESS. REMEMBER, HIS ENTIRE REALITY IS SHAPED BY UNVERIFIED CUSTOMER ANECDOTES.

I HEARD A RUMOR OF A STORY OF AN ALLEGED FOCUS GROUP WHERE A QUOTE TAKEN OUT OF CONTEXT INDICATES YOU'RE NOT BECOMING A WEASEL.

I'M NOT?!

YIPEEE!

OUR NEW DRESS POLICY AT WORK ALLOWS CASUAL CLOTHES ON FRIDAYS.

THAT'S GOOD, BECAUSE STUDIES HAVE SHOWN THAT FRIDAYS ARE THE ONLY SAFE DAY TO DRESS CASUALLY; ANY OTHER DAY WOULD CAUSE A STOCK PLUNGE.

IS IT JUST ME OR IS THAT POLICY STUPID?

THAT'S NOT AN "OR" QUESTION.

I WANT US TO HAVE THE SAME KIND OF TEAMWORK AS THE EGYPTIANS WHO BUILT THE PYRAMIDS!

SOME SCHOLARS BELIEVE THE PYRAMIDS WERE BUILT BY SLAVES.

BUT THERE'S SOME DOUBT; THAT'S ALL I'M SHOOTING FOR.

I THINK THEY WERE GUIDED BY UFOs TOO.

83

86

93

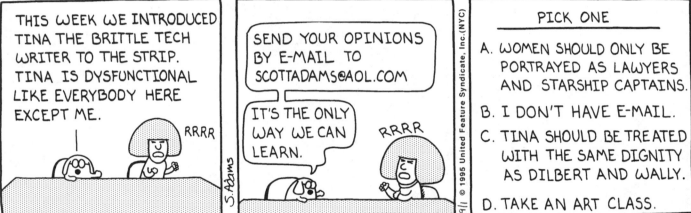

95

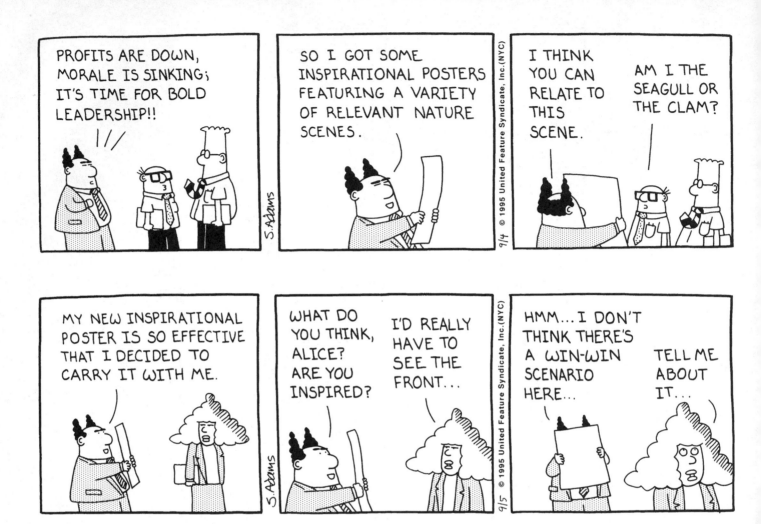

113